FIRST-TIME HOMEBUYER HANDBOOK

From Credit to Closing and Beyond

from *Platinum* Realtor

Tysharda "Ty" Thomas

Contents

Testimonials

"I have purchased several pieces of real estate in the last 20+ years. My most recent purchase was with Tysharda. I could tell from the first time we met at a property showing Ty was different. She exuded a genuine "client care" which is hard to find. I found that I could trust her opinion and her expertise. As I searched through multiple listings to find the right investment property, Tysharda was patient, forthright, responsive, and attentive. She quickly picked up on what I was looking for and what price point would be comfortable. Without a doubt, Ty's experience and genuine caring personality was most certainly beneficial in my finding the exact right property in a really great location at a really great price. #team_ty."

Denise M. Williams

"I met Tysharda Thomas at New 2 U Homes in 2010 when she called to obtain special first-time homebuyer mortgage information for her customers. She is passionate about learning all that she can about the best mortgage solutions for her clients. Tysharda understands that everyone wants to buy a house, but there is a lot of hard work that goes into getting ready financially and emotionally. She is more than just a realtor. She is a mentor, she is a teacher, and she is a friend to her clients. She is professional, honest, trustworthy, and unwavering in her mission to help customers find the right house. Whether it is your first house, or your forever home, Tysharda Thomas will work tirelessly on your behalf to make the dream of homeownership a reality."

Laura Smith, Mortgage Loan Officer
Genesee Regional Bank

"When searching for a home, the first thing one should consider and take into account is whom they will entrust to take them through the purchasing process. This is something that should not be taken lightly. It is important that whomever you choose is someone that you trust. The aforementioned is why I chose New 2 U Homes as my real estate service company.

When I had the opportunity to purchase my second home, I will make the same choice once again. My home buying process from start to finish was seamless. The Thomas's truly went above and beyond to ensure my experience was a pleasurable one. Purchasing your first home is not only an investment but will become part of your life's canvas. There were certain things that I required, and if a property did not have, were deal breakers for me. The Thomas's knew this and made sure that they did not recommend any properties that did not meet my needs. They take the term "Buyer's Agent" seriously and truly advocate for what their buyers want.

Will there be hurdles along the way? Yes! Nothing in life worth having will come easy, nor will it be "given" to you. However, it is important that you trust your realtor and give them the authority they need to make the important and necessary decisions to advocate for you. At one point during my buying process, right when we thought we were at the end of the finish line, the house I had in contract appraised lower than the selling price. At that point, the seller asked that I increase my out of pocket investment to make up the difference, which I was not willing to do. This is where I trusted Chris and Ty to do exactly what they were hired to do, advocate for me. When Chris called me up to deliver the news, he asked, "What would you like to do?" My response was, I am not going to be married to an opportunity, either they come down on the price or just like you found me this home, we will find another. It all worked out in the end because I trusted Chris and Ty to do exactly what they are experts in doing, and that is being THE BEST, exclusive buyer's agents in our region"

Ebony Miller-Wesley

"I began my home buying journey in a new city and with no understanding of how buying a home worked. I had only been living in Monroe County for 2 years and didn't know much. I had the pleasure of working with Mrs. Tysharda Thomas from New2UHomes and the experience changed my life. As a first-time home buyer there is a lot of information thrown at you in what seems like a very short period of time. Mrs. Thomas took the time to make sure I understood everything. She was kind and patient with me and helped me to learn about the city of Rochester and the surrounding towns. She wanted to make sure I was an informed buyer. She went the extra mile to show me I was not just a client who needed to hurry up and buy a home. She was more concerned with my happiness than me closing on a house. Mrs. Thomas was more than a real estate agent trying to sell me a house, she became family. How many people can say they sat at the table with their real estate agent and shared a meal? How many people can say they held hands with their real estate agent and prayed about next steps and moving forward. If you are looking to enjoy the process of buying a home, not just getting a house, look no further than Mrs. Tysharda Thomas of New2UHomes. You won't be disappointed!"

Gena W.

New 2 U Homes Accomplishments

- ❖ 2019 Special Mayoral Recognition

- ❖ 2019 Black Business ROC Award

- ❖ 2018 Tysharda Thomas- Bain Stephen Community Excellence Award

- ❖ 2016 Sales Master Platinum Award-Greater Rochester Association of REALTORS

- ❖ 2015 Sales Master Platinum Award-Greater Rochester Association of REALTORS

- ❖ 2015 Christopher Thomas- Featured in Top Agent Magazine New York Edition

- ❖ 2014 Sales Master Platinum Award-Greater Rochester Association of REALTORS

- ❖ 2013 Sales Master Gold Award-Greater Rochester Association of REALTORS

Introduction

New 2 U Homes was founded in 2008 by Christopher and Tysharda Thomas who saw a need to assist first-generation homebuyers through the home buying process from credit to closing and beyond. Christopher purchased his first home at the age of 18 and has been passionate about real estate ever since. Since 2008, New 2 U Homes has grown tremendously and is recognized as one of the best brokerages in Rochester, NY. Their success is credited to their dedication to personalization of the home buying experience for each client. Future ventures include developing communities that improve the lives of minority and disadvantaged individuals. New 2 U Homes is not limited to helping first time buyers, the agency also specializes in commercial real estate including multi-family, mixed-use, retail, and religious properties.

New 2 U Homes saw the necessity for first time homebuyers to have someone in their corner advocating on their behalf. They also saw that there was a great need for home buyer's education, advocacy, and a familiar face to be there throughout the process.

Ty Thomas joined her husband full-time in 2009 after leaving a career of teaching and helping troubled youth. New 2 U Homes started as a mobile office, but the Thomas' quickly realized that a central location was necessary. A brick and mortar allowed clients to receive personalized services including monthly homebuyer education classes. Since joining, Ty has helped New 2 U Homes grow enormously by bringing her case-management background to the home buying process thereby assisting a lot more clients.

New 2 U Homes is a full-service brokerage like no other. They specialize in listening to their buyers and sellers, helping buyers find the perfect property at the best value possible. New 2 U Homes also helps sellers accomplish their goals quickly and for the highest price. New 2 U Homes is an all-inclusive real-estate brokerage which assists their clients from credit to closing. They provide education for their buyers, assist with first-time homebuyer grant programs, and attend every closing possible once their buyers reach the finish line. They love seeing the pride and joy in the faces of their clients when they hand them their keys at the closing table.

In 2014, New 2 U Homes was recognized by the Greater Rochester Area of Realtors for obtaining platinum status (the highest level of sales achievement a REALTOR ® can obtain. New 2 U Homes is the first African American independently owned real estate brokerage in Rochester, NY to achieve platinum status.

New 2 U Homes' mission is to "Make Rochester a better place by helping motivated people achieve their real estate goals". They work tirelessly to see as many people as possible become homeowners.

Why Was I Inspired to Write This Book?

When I purchased my first home in 2003, I had absolutely no idea what I was doing. When I closed on that home, I still had no idea WHAT I HAD DONE. I am hoping that this book takes the unknown out of the entire homeownership process. I want to create a world of informed and knowledgeable first-time homebuyers who inevitably become first-time homeowners.

Why Should You Read This Book?

If you are a first-time homebuyer, especially a first-generation buyer, this book is for you! It will give you an in-depth look at the process of homeownership from credit to closing and beyond.

What You Will Gain from This Book?

Reading this book will take the fear out of the homebuying and homeownership process and replace it with an undeniable sense of relief and empowerment. My goal is to simplify the homebuying process which can be confusing and tedious. After completing this book, you will have a journal that chronicles your accomplishments throughout the journey to homeownership.

The Definition of a First-Time Homebuyer

An individual who has had no ownership in a principal residence during the 3-year period ending on the date of purchase of the property. This includes a spouse (if either meets the above criteria, they are considered first-time homebuyers).

One of the Federal Housing Administration's primary criteria is whether you've owned a home before. If you've never owned a home, you're considered a first-time homebuyer. However, you can be a previous homeowner and still qualify as a first-time homebuyer. According to the FHA, you can do so if you have not been an owner in a primary residence for at least three years leading up to your purchase. In this case, you and a spouse are treated separately. If you've owned a home but your spouse has not, then you can buy a home together as first-time homebuyers.

Myths & Legends

Throughout my 11-year real estate career, I have seen a lot and heard a lot, my favorites are what I like to call the myths & legends.

Here are a few misconceptions that some first-time homebuyers have:

Myth: If you live on a corner lot that intersects two streets you pay double taxes.

Fact: Property taxes are based on your property assessment. If your lot is larger than a neighboring property your taxes may be higher, however, if your lot is around the same size that will not affect your taxes.

A low assessment means that your taxes will be lower and cause your overall mortgage to be less.

Myth: As a first-time homebuyer I should look at, at least 10 homes before I decide.

Fact: When you walk into your home you will know! A home calls out to you and pulls on your heartstrings, whether that is the first home or the 11th home, it does not matter. The home that you saw today and want to think about someone else saw yesterday and they are already writing an offer.

Myth: If you have a pre-qualification or pre-approval for $100,000 but you find a home for $80,000 you can take the remaining $20,000 and use it for updates or home improvements.

Fact: Unless you are obtaining a rehab loan you are only able to borrow the amount that you need from the bank for that home. A rehab loan assists the buyer with the purchase of the home plus the cost of repairs.

Myth: If you owe federal or state taxes but get on a payment plan you can still move forward with purchasing a home and obtaining a mortgage.

Fact: Depending on the type of mortgage you are applying for you need to meet certain criteria. The lender will look for proof that you have a valid agreement with the IRS and that you have made at least one payment. However, if you have a tax lien with the IRS you cannot move forward with a mortgage (it is considered a debt and it must be paid before you can obtain a mortgage). This payment WILL be counted in your debt to income ratio.

Myth: The higher your credit score, the lower your interest rate.

Fact: A higher credit score does sometimes dictate a lower interest rate; however, it depends on the mortgage program.

Myth: If my student loans are in deferment or forbearance, they will not be counted against me when qualifying me for a mortgage.

Fact: In most cases the lender/bank will require a letter stating what your estimated monthly payment will be in the future. This estimation is included in your debt-to-income ratio.

Myth: I can get an amazing deal to purchase a home valued at $200,000 for $70,000 with little or no effort.

Fact: You must but be prepared to roll up your sleeves and do the work yourself or have a great team of professionals help you!

Home Buying Tips

Welcome to New 2 U Homes!

Our goal at New 2 U Homes is to assist you with the home-buying process from start to finish. As we discuss the process, please take a moment to fill in the information as it is presented. We look forward to taking this journey with you!

Our Mission is to help MOTIVATED people achieve their Real Estate Goals.

Real Estate in a Nutshell

How does the process of selling a home begin?
- Who represents the seller?
  _____
- Who represents the buyer ?
  _____

Before You Purchase We Will:

- Assist with credit repair and preparation
- Work with you to attain your mortgage Pre-approval
- Assist you with all grant applications

Mortgage Requirements

In order to qualify for a Mortgage you will need:

1. _____
2. _____
3. _____
4. _____

When You Are Pre-approved We Will:

SEARCH FOR AND FIND YOUR PERFECT HOME
- Help you Negotiate the BEST possible price and terms
- Walk hand in hand through your home inspection
- Do a final inspection and make sure you get your KEYS!!!

Grants/Savings/Gift

How I will obtain closing costs:

- _____
- _____
- _____

After You Close We Will:

- Welcome you to the New 2 U Homes Family
- Be A Lifelong resource for ALL of your Real Estate needs!

My Personal Goals

_____

_____

Chapter 1

Agency

"Loyalty is hard to find,

trust is easy to lose

actions speak louder than words"

- Anonymous

History of Buyer's Agency

Buyer's Agency was established in 1992, until then everyone involved in the real estate process worked for the seller. A seller would hire an agent to list their home known as a listing agent (seller's agent). The listing agent would represent the seller to get them the best price and terms for the sale. Once the listing agent placed that home on the MLS (Multiple Listing System) (a database where other agents search for listings), it became an offer of cooperation (an open invitation to other brokers to sell a property listed by another broker). The agent could then present a qualified buyer to purchase the home. However, everyone in the transaction was working for whom? The seller. That's why the term "Seller is King" was used, the seller paid the commissions, and everyone was working to sell the home for the benefit of the seller.

In 1992, the Buyer's Agency was established. The buyer had no representation in the transaction and therefore had no protection, except for the goodwill and integrity of his agents. When Buyer's

Agency was established this designated someone to work directly on behalf of the buyer.

According to the REALTOR ® Code of Ethics, your Buyer's Agent owes you:

Obedience: Must obey legal instructions of a client.

Loyalty: Put client's interests above others, even your own.

Disclosure: Disclose all material facts pertinent to the transaction.

Confidentiality: Keep client information confidential, even after closing.

Accountability: Account for all monies and property entrusted to you by your client.

Reasonable Care: Provide clients quality and knowledgeable service.

Your agent should be as reliable as an **OLD CAR** (well the way they used to make them anyway). You could depend on it to get up and go no matter how old it was. Regardless that the muffler may be loud, and oil may be leaking but it still got you from Point A to Point B.

Why Use a Buyer's Agent?

By default, all real estate agents *represent* and *owe* their *fiduciary* (confidence or trust, relating to a duty of acting in good faith regarding the interests of another) responsibilities to the **SELLER** during any real estate transaction.

As a Buyer, you can elect to have a **BUYER'S AGENT** who represents YOU and is able to put your interests above all others.

Example Scenario:

You are working with an agent who shows you 25 different homes over three weekends. The Agent buys you lunch twice, knows all four of your children by name as well as all your personal likes and dislikes, but does not offer **Buyer Agency**. You feel comfortable with the agent revealing important personal information.

Without **Buyer Agency**, "your" agent represents and owes loyalty to every one of those 25 Sellers- and not to you. Any information you reveal to the agent must be relayed to the sellers.

Why Do I Need Representation?

If the agent represents the seller, he/she cannot disclose anything that would be detrimental to the seller's position (i.e. reason for selling, lowest price the seller would accept, market/neighborhood conditions that would give you an advantage, etc.).

Having a BUYER'S AGENT represent you gives you several advantages:

- Access to information that may give you the upper hand in the transaction.
- Access to a Comparative Market Analysis (CMA) that shows what price similar properties have been listed and sold for.
- Access to information about property value trends.

What If You Decide to Part Ways with an Agent?

If you ever feel like the relationship between you and your agent just isn't working out, ask yourself a few questions first:

- Does the agent have my best interest at heart?
- How can you help your agent help you?
- Have you given the agent all the necessary criteria to serve you and find your home? (amenities, location, price point that you feel comfortable with, any other underlying factors such as crime statistics, neighborhood features, etc.?).

If you've answered YES to all of these questions and you still feel as though you may want to part ways, the proper way to do this is to find out if you've signed a Buyer's Agency Agreement. If so, review the agreement for your options to end the agreement. I have spent hours on the phone with clients who want to "switch" agents. I asked the client if he/she has done his/her part as well. I know how this industry can be and how difficult it can be to serve clients wholeheartedly, while balancing multiple offers juggling showing schedules and managing listings.

Chapter 2

Credit Do's & Don'ts

"A good financial plan is a road map that shows us exactly how the choices we make today will affect our future."

- Alexa Von Tobel

Tips for Prepping your Credit for Purchase

Do obtain your credit scores from the three major credit bureaus (Experian, Equifax, and TransUnion). When you are ready to purchase allowing a lender (bank) to pull your credit is the best way to do this. A lender cannot utilize a credit report from another lender. This initial credit pull is necessary to create your entire picture and give realistic expectations for your home buying journey.

Do pay all bills on-time. Avoid late payments and skipped payments. Automatic payments are a great way to achieve this! Even one late payment can delay your opportunity to purchase a home for 12-months.

Do pay down balances owed on credit cards and other month-to-month obligations to decrease your debt to income ratio. A good rule of thumb is keeping your cards at about 20-30% utilization.

Do stop using your credit cards until after you close on your home.

Do demand that negative credit more than 7 years old be removed from your credit report.

Do maintain 3-4 Credit Tradelines: credit cards (secured or unsecured), auto loans, student loans, or personal loans (short-term, long-term, secured, or unsecured).

Do save a few months of mortgage payments to avoid financial stress in the event of unforeseen circumstances (job loss/change, mechanical/structural issues).

Do save money for closing costs and down payment. You will not receive grants until you are at the closing table. There are upfront costs associated with getting into contract and closing such as the earnest money deposit, inspection fee, mortgage/appraisal fee, and homeowner's insurance.

Do NOT co-sign under any circumstances unless you can comfortably pay the entire debt yourself. There is no way to co-sign without affecting your credit. If someone tells you otherwise, that's not true (i.e. If you co-sign for furniture, it's yours, even if it's not at your house. If you co-sign for a vehicle for someone, you might as well drive it yourself.

Do NOT max out your credit cards. (30% utilization is a good rule of thumb).

Do NOT open numerous credit accounts at the same time (i.e. store credit cards). If you are trying to build your credit, consult with your lender (loan officer or mortgage broker) on how to increase your score. However, if you are shopping around for a mortgage, do it quickly.

Do NOT save cash at home underneath your mattress. This money cannot be used towards closing. The bank wants to know where all your funds are coming from whether it's payroll, taxes, a gift from a relative, etc. Also, your money needs to be in a bank account for at least 3 months to be considered "seasoned".

Do NOT close your credit cards when you pay them off.

Do NOT use one credit card to pay off another.

Monthly Expenses

Housing	Current	Proposed
Cable/Satellite		
Gas & Electric		
Internet		
Phone (Cell/Landline)		
Rent		
Renter's Insurance		
Water/Garbage/Sewer		
Food	Current	Proposed
Alcohol		
Coffee		
Dining Out		

	Current	Proposed
Food at Work/School		
Other		
Medical	Current	Proposed
Dentist/Orthodontist		
Doctor Co-pays		
Health/Dental/Vision Insurance		
Life Disability Insurance		
Optometrist/Lenses		
Other		
Prescriptions		
Transportation	Current	Proposed
Auto Insurance		
Car Payment # 1		
Car Payment # 2		

DMV Registration/Inspection		
Gasoline/Oil		
Maintenance/Repairs		
Public Transportation		
Obligations	Current	Proposed
Child Support/Alimony/Palimony		
Student Loans		
Other		
Other		
Other		
Personal	Current	Proposed
Beauty/Barber		
Clothing/Jewelry		
Lashes/Brows/Beard		

Laundry/Dry Cleaning		
Manicure/Pedicure		
Other		
Other		
Other		
Other		
Entertainment	Current	Proposed
Books/Magazine/Newspaper		
Gym Membership		
Movies/Concerts/Theater		
Netflix/Hulu/Memberships		
Sports/Hobbies		
Vacations/Travel		
Miscellaneous	Current	Proposed
Childcare		

Holiday/Birthday/Gifts		
Pet Care		
Religious Contributions/Tithes		
Tuition		
Other		
Savings	Current	Proposed
Emergency Savings		

Notes

_____

_____

_____

_____

_____

_____

Current Debts

(Please list all debts)

Name of Creditor	Account #	Months Late	Current Balance	Current Payment	Interest Rate
Ex. Credit Card	XXXX568	1	$2000	$34	24.5%

Name of Creditor	Account #	Months Late	Current Balance	Current Payment	Interest Rate

Notes

_____

_____

_____

_____

_____

_____

_____

_____

_____

_____

_____

_____

_____

_____

_____

_____

_____

Assets: Monthly Income

Monthly Income	Gross Income	Net Income	Partner Income	Partner Net
Child Support/Alimony/ Palimony				
Government Assistance				
Income Source/Employer				
Part-Time Employment				
Rental Income				
Retirement/Pension				
Social Security				
Support Family/Friends				
Unemployment				

Other Income				
Other Income				
Other Income				
Other Income				
Total Income				

Notes

_____

_____

_____

_____

_____

_____

_____

_____

_____

_____

_____

Assets & Liabilities

Home Mortgage	Present Value	Amount Owed	Monthly Payment
401(k)/403(b) Loan			
Other Mortgage/HELOC			
Property/Land Second Mortgage			
Vehicle Payment #1			
Vehicle Payment #2			
Other Payments			
Other Payments			
Total Assets & Liabilities			

Notes

_____

_____

_____

_____

_____

_____

_____

_____

_____

_____

_____

_____

_____

_____

_____

_____

_____

_____

Other Investments

Home Mortgage	Present Value	Monthly Contribution	Proposed Contribution
401(k)/403(b) Contribution			
Cash Value Life Insurance			
IRA			
Money Market/Stocks/CD			
Savings Account			
Other Investments			
Other Investments			
Other Investments			

Other Investments			
Total Investments			

Notes

_____

_____

_____

_____

_____

_____

_____

_____

_____

_____

_____

_____

_____

_____

Let's Talk Trade Lines

Trade lines are items that you pay monthly that are reported to one of the three major Credit reporting agencies (Experian, TransUnion, and Equifax). Some examples of credit trade lines are auto loans, student loans and credit cards, both secured and unsecured.

Alternative trade lines can be paid out of your checking account monthly. Sometimes the bank can use 12 months of bank statements to highlight your payment history of these items. These payments can provide additional credit history to the underwriter to obtain a mortgage approval. Some examples of alternative credit include gas and electric, cable, car insurance, life insurance, etc.

On-time payments for direct and alternative trade lines is most important when applying for a mortgage. Depending on the type of mortgage you are attempting to acquire banks may want to see between 12-18 months of positive payment history with **NO LATE PAYMENTS.**

It's okay, BREATHE if you have not been doing this...start now.

List Your Current Trade Lines

Trade Line	Limit	Balance	Goal Balance	Month Positive Payments	Current Payment
Ex. Credit Card	$1000	$500	$0	2 years	$35

Trade Line	Limit	Balance	Goal Balance	Month Positive Payments	Current Payment
Ex. Credit Card	$1000	$500	$0	2 years	$35

What current habits are positively affecting your credit?

_____

_____

_____

What habits are negatively affecting your credit?

_____

_____

_____

"You Can't Get Out of Debt While Keeping the Same Lifestyle That Got You There."

- Dave Ramsey

Chapter 3

Selecting

Your Team

"The Strength of the Team is Each
Individual Member. The Strength of
Each Member is the Team."

-Phil Jackson

Why is choosing your team the most important part of your home buying process?

Without a solid team everything crumbles. Each person's job is significant in a real estate transaction. From the real estate professional to the real estate attorney, each role is pivotal in the home buying process.

Who Makes up Your Team?

Real Estate Professional/REALTOR®: assists you with finding a home, putting in an offer, and explaining the contract to you in depth, walking you through the contract and helping you with the home purchase process until you obtain those keys.

Licensed Engineer/Home Inspector: the individual who provides a thorough assessment of the home as a whole such as electrical systems, plumbing, structural, and latent defects (things that you cannot see with the naked eye) and to answer any questions regarding the inspection.

Mortgage Professional/Loan Officer/Mortgage Broker: pre-qualifies/pre-approves you for a mortgage, explains what you qualify for, how much you need for closing, processes your mortgage application, walks you through commitment and the entire mortgage process.

Real Estate Attorney: An attorney who specializes in real estate is essential...I'm not knocking family malpractice or general practice attorneys at all. I am merely saying that you want an attorney who specializes in real estate from day-to-day and is proficient in real estate. Your real estate attorney will walk you through the purchase contract before they approve it. Additionally, your attorney will conduct a title search (liens and encumbrances, see glossary) and review any leases or rental agreements tied to the property.

Insurance Agent: Homeowner's insurance like renter's insurance is important for many reasons. Not only does it protect the investment (which the bank wants), it also protects you in the long run. In many states, including New York State, you cannot close on your home without homeowner's insurance.

Who Makes Up Your Team?

Real Estate Professional/Realtor®:

_____

Mortgage Professional/Loan Officer/Mortgage
Broker: _____

Licensed Engineer/Home Inspector:

_____

Real Estate Attorney: _____

Insurance Agent: _____

Notes

_____

_____

_____

_____

_____

_____

Chapter 4
Mortgage Requirements

"Home is Where the Mortgage Is."

-Billy Connolly

What Are the 4 Major Things that You Need to Be "Mortgage-Able?"

1. 3-4 Credit Tradelines: (i.e. Student loans, Auto loans, Credit cards, etc.)

   - *Quick Refresher-* There is another type of tradeline called an **Alternative Tradeline** which can be used if a person doesn't have strong enough credit history. Alternative trade lines are anything that you pay out of your bank account for 12-18 months or longer (i.e. monthly utility bills, phone bills, gym memberships and yes even Amazon Prime or Netflix). Typically, lenders are looking for a bill that is at least $20 per month with ABSOLUTELY no missed payments. Automatic payments are the best way to ensure that you can prove this. The lenders want to see your consistency in paying those bills.

   - The **most important** alternative tradeline is your **RENT**! Think about it. If the bank sees that you can afford a $1300 payment monthly for a long period of time, what will stop them from lending you $130,000 for a mortgage? Lenders can do a verification of rental for apartment complexes. Lenders contact the property management company, however, it's best you show your own 12-18 months of bank statements highlighting your rental payment each month. For example, if your rent is $800 a month and there is a withdrawal for $800 a month coming out of your checking account, the banks can use that as proof. If you pay cash one month or utilize another account this negates this tradeline.

2. **Two-years of Verifiable Income**: (employment, retirement, disability, etc.) Anything that you file on your taxes for two years counts as verifiable income. If you are self-employed you **MUST** file taxes on your business for two years or it cannot be included in your income when qualifying you for a mortgage. Please check with your local lender. Banks may view this differently if you've just graduated from college and

obtained a job in your field or have part-time employment for a year or more. It depends on the loan type and the lender.

3. **Credit Score 660 or above**: Can you purchase a home with a lower score?

   Yes, however you want to be in the best financial place possible when making one of the largest purchases that you will ever make in your life. If your score is lower than 660, if anything hits your credit during the transaction it WILL bring your score down. As a result, the bank will deny your loan if it is lower than the required credit score for that lending institution. Please remember that the score depends on the mortgage type (FHA or Conventional) and/or the lender.

4. **No Collections or Judgments**: Bottom line, the bank does not want to see that you owe anyone who could possibly come after you for money or attempt to place a lien on your property. Collections and judgments also show the bank that you are not responsible with credit. The bank wants to

see that you are using credit as a tool. Banks are, however, more lenient with medical collections. Remember, banks want to see that you have credit and are using it wisely.

Quick Reference on Loan Types

FHA (Federal Housing Administration)**:** A government-backed loan with less restrictive qualifications. FHA requires 3.5% down payment plus closing costs.

Conventional: A non-government backed loan with more stringent guidelines. Conventional loans require 3-5% down payment plus closing costs.

VA Loan: Loans backed by the United States Department of Veterans Affairs (VA) and reserved for veterans. VA Loans require 0% down plus closing costs.

Most sellers prefer conventional loans to FHA Loans due to the rigorous appraisals that an FHA loan may entail.

Pre-Approval Checklist

(Have these items with you when applying for a mortgage)

- ☐ Alimony/Palimony Documentation
- ☐ Bank Statements
- ☐ Child Support
- ☐ Last Two Years Taxes
- ☐ Last Two Years W-2's
  or 1099's (self-employed)
- ☐ Pay Stubs & Income Documentation
- ☐ Retirement Savings
- ☐ SSI or SSD Income

Chapter 5
What You
Can Afford
vs. What
You Want

"It's Not How Big a House is, It's How Happy the Home Is."

- Author Unknown

We always tell our buyers that the bank may qualify you for any amount, but you must know what you are comfortable with for a monthly mortgage payment. It can be the difference between you eating ramen noodles four nights out of the week, going on an international vacation once a year or even putting your child through college.

To figure out your comfort level consider what you currently pay for rent. Are you struggling? Is it a breeze? Many first-time buyers hear that mortgages are less than rent so they come to us with all their heart's desires wanting to pay considerably LESS than their rent. Your mortgage can indeed be less than rent depending on what type of home you want, how many bedrooms and baths, amenities, location, and taxes. However, it's not guaranteed.

Also, if you are receiving temporary income from child support, alimony or some other form of verifiable income temporarily, picture your situation without that money coming in and be sure that you can afford the mortgage without the additional income. Something else to contemplate is whether you are purchasing with a significant other, a family member, or solely on your own.

These are all things to take into consideration when looking at how much you can comfortably afford.

As a first-time homebuyer, it is essential to make a list of what you want in your first home vs. your dream home/forever home. Those are two separate things for most people which leads us to our next chapter on identifying a property. For example, you can have the en suite bathroom, 2.5 car garage and walk-in closet in the next home, not your first one. If you think about this now it can save you a ton of stress and heartache when shopping for your first home.

WANTS VS. NEEDS

Chapter 6
Identifying
A Property

"I Don't Like Dreams or Reality. I Like When Dreams Become Reality because That Is My Life."

-John Paul Gaultier

Location...Location...Location

I'm sure you've heard the clichés. You can't move your home (unless it's a mobile home). You can't choose your neighbors. You're buying the home and the entire neighborhood.

Well.... it's ALL TRUE. Location is one of the most important factors that should come into play during the home buying process. Is the neighborhood "safe"? How close is it to work, church, grocery stores, gym, lash tech, nail salon, etc.? Is it a quiet neighborhood, is it a seasoned neighborhood, or an up and coming neighborhood? School districts play an important role if you have children or plan to start a family.

Check your local crime watcher, city, and county websites for accurate and up-to-date information on neighborhoods.

Key Decision Makers

When shopping for a home, depending on whether you are purchasing it alone or with someone, you want to ensure the key people attend as many showings as possible. If they can make it to every single showing, even better. There is nothing worse than viewing a home on your own and wanting to return to that home with your spouse or parent and that home no longer being available. Remember, the home that you saw today and wanted to think about, someone else saw yesterday and they are currently writing an offer. Don't let your first home slip through your fingers due to lack of planning.

Cosmetic vs. Structural

Cosmetic improvements are normally items that you can live with such as paint, wallpaper, or carpet. A fresh coat of paint and ripping up carpet can work wonders for a home! There are so many DIY home improvements, books and videos that can walk you through the process to save money if you do not want to pay a contractor.

Structural improvements such as bathrooms, kitchens, new roofs, or windows are larger ticket items that a first-time homebuyer may not be able to tackle. When searching for a home it is important to know if a home is being sold "as-is". Ask if the seller will do repairs or address concerns. This may come up at the time of inspection or prior to closing but the buyer needs to know that well in advance. These improvements may require a contractor or someone who is skilled in the trade.

The Feeling

Ask anyone that you know that owns a home. There is an undeniable feeling that you get when you walk into YOUR HOME. It is as if the home is truly pulling on your heartstrings.

Personally, I live for that look on my client's face. That feeling can occur in the very first home that you see or the 12th home that you see. There is no magic number. Whatever you do, don't ignore the feeling. Don't let anyone tell you that it is too soon nor that you should hold off or look at more homes.

Remember, an amazing agent can home in on your search criteria and narrow it down in a precise manner, but it is up to you to leap over that threshold to homeownership.

Notes

_____

_____

_____

_____

_____

_____

_____

_____

_____

_____

_____

_____

_____

_____

_____

_____

_____

Chapter 7

Home

Purchase

Process

"Nothing in Life Comes Easy.
Everything Comes with a Sacrifice."

-Rihanna

Are You Ready to Buy?

How do you know when you are ready to start viewing homes?

There are so many times when it seems that out of the blue, I receive that infamous call or email stating that a buyer is "ready" and would like to schedule a showing of a home. When I speak to the buyer it is revealed that he or she hasn't spoken to a loan officer or been pre-qualified or pre-approved. Not only is this a disservice to the seller who thinks you are ready, but it is also a disservice to you because you may fall in love with a home you are not in position to write an offer or even qualify for. Let us not fail to mention the real estate professional who takes the time to schedule the showing and get you into the home.

We tell our buyers to be equipped, fully, and ready to "fight" for that home. To do so you must meet with a mortgage professional to see where you stand. What do you qualify for? Are you ready now or do you need a little more time to prepare? Be advised, postponing home ownership is not the end of the world.

Pre-Qualification vs. Pre-Approval

In the eyes of a seller and listing agent, a pre-approval is always better than a pre-qualification letter. You can obtain a pre-qualification from just about anywhere. However, a pre-approval letter carries more weight because a loan officer/mortgage professional needs to vet you (taxes, w-2's, pay stubs or any other proof of income). We tell our buyers to be armed and ready with your pre-approval in hand during a busy homebuying season.

Applying for Grants

There are a plethora of grants and assistance for first time homebuyers. Please check with your local city, county, and state to inquire about and apply for any grants that you may qualify for.

Eligibility may be determined by household income, neighborhood, and companies that may offer employer assisted housing grants.

House Hunting!

Rate each home on a scale of 1 to 5, 1 being the least favorable to 5 being the most favorable:

Address: _____

Area/Convenience	
Bath	
Bedroom Size/Closet Space	
Curb Appeal / Yard	
Interior Space	
Kitchen	
WOW FACTOR!	

Address: _____

Area/Convenience	
Bath	
Bedroom/Closet Space	
Curb Appeal / Yard	
Interior Space	
Kitchen	
WOW FACTOR!	

Address: _____

Area/Convenience	
Bath	
Bedroom Size/Closet Space	
Curb Appeal / Yard	
Interior Space	
Kitchen	
WOW FACTOR!	

Address: _____

Area/Convenience	
Bath	
Bedroom Size/Closet Space	
Curb Appeal / Yard	
Interior Space	
Kitchen	
WOW FACTOR!	

Address: _____

Area/Convenience	
Bath	
Bedroom Size/Closet Space	
Curb Appeal / Yard	
Interior Space	
Kitchen	
WOW FACTOR!	

Home Vision Board

Utilize this Space to Do a Mini Vision Board of Your Dream Home

Habakkuk 2:2

"And the LORD answered me, and said, Write the vision, and make it plain upon tables, that he may run that readeth it."

Important Must-Knows

Mortgage Application Process

When the buyer meets with the lender (loan officer) and applies for their mortgage, the buyer submits all their documents for the pre-approval process. The buyer may pay for their appraisal/mortgage application fee at that time as well (varies by loan type and lender).

Appraisal vs. Assessment

Potential buyers confuse the property assessment (the value of the property based on taxes) with the property appraisal (the value of the property based on a professional appraiser's opinion of what the home would sell for on an open market). The value of the home is determined when the bank appraiser observes your potential home to ensure that it is worth what you are paying for it. They consider the price of similar homes. The homes in the comparison group are known as comps.

Commitment

Once the lender (bank) has agreed to give you the mortgage, you move towards final conditions to clear your mortgage to close. Final conditions may include verification of employment, updated pay stubs, bank statements, and proof of homeowner's insurance

Clear to Close

Once the lender (bank) gives you a final clear to close, attorneys schedule your closing. The buyer's attorney and the seller's attorney, the bank, and grant organizations must be on board to schedule.

Final Walk-Through

Your final walkthrough is important for many reasons. It's the last opportunity to see the home before closing and to make sure that it's still in the condition that you saw it in upon inspection or better. Your REALTOR ® will schedule your final walkthrough within 24-48 hours prior to closing. Things to take with you (Trulia):

- Your final contract. Your contract will note what should and should not be in the house

when you buy it. (I.e. appliances, window treatments, and shelving.
- Notepad. In addition to your final walkthrough checklist, you'll want plenty of paper to jot down any questions or observations.
- Phone. Use your phone to take pictures of anything you want to make a record of.
- Phone charger. Sure, you don't want your phone to die, but more importantly, the charger could come in handy if you need to confirm that the electrical outlets are functional.
- Inspection summary. It's important to double-check that all repairs have been completed as promised.
- Your real estate agent.

Final Walk-Through Checklist

- ☐ Have all required repairs been made?
- ☐ Have all repair receipts and warranties been provided?
- ☐ Check the basement for dampness or mold that may have not been apparent depending on the season.

- ☐ Is the included personal property in place and in working order?
- ☐ Are all windows and doors in good working order?
- ☐ Are these areas free of water damage or mold? (Kitchen, Bathrooms, Refrigerator, Washer/Dryer, Water Heater)
- ☐ Is there damage to interior floors, walls, or ceilings?
- ☐ Check plumbing, flush toilets, fill sinks. Is every drain working properly?
- ☐ Electrical: Are all lights working? Plate covers? GFCI (Ground Fault Circuit Interrupter) Outlets?
- ☐ Exterior: make sure the roof, siding and landscaping are as expected.
- ☐ Broom Clean (clean and free from any large items that were not required to remain on site per any agreement set forth between buyer and seller)- This definition varies by person

Pre-Closing

- ☐ Change utilities from the seller to your name.
- ☐ Change your mailing address. You would be surprised how many people forget to do this and continue to place orders. There's nothing like ordering a new pair of shoes and wondering what happened to them.

Closing

- Remember to bring your id, find out 24-48 hours prior what your final numbers are, and how many checks you need and to whom they must be made out to.

Most likely, these checks will need to be certified checks. Check with your attorney.

Post-Closing

- ☐ Change locks.
- ☐ Update home alarm codes.

Quick Q&A

Question: If the inspector finds an issue with the house but the seller can't or won't fix it, can I cancel the contract and get my money back from the inspection?

Answer: No, because the inspector did the job, he/she was hired to do.

Question: What if the home inspection reveals something costly, would I be responsible for it?

Answer: The home inspection protects the buyer. It is another contingency per your contract and another level of negotiation for your agent.

For example, the home may be listed "as-is". What does "as-is" mean? As-is means there are minor defects in the home or there could be glaring defects such as the home needs a new roof or furnace. In this case, the seller either doesn't have the funds to repair before listing or merely does not want to, these defects decrease the cost of the property.

Notes

_____

_____

_____

_____

_____

_____

_____

_____

_____

_____

Chapter 8

You Own A Home...

Now What?

"Opportunity is Missed by Most People Because it is Dressed in Overalls and Looks Like Work."

-Thomas Edison

You're Finally a Homeowner...Congratulations!

There is something to be said about being a responsible homeowner. Check with your local city or county for any tax exemptions that you may qualify for. Also, research grants such as lead abatements or home improvement grants post-purchase.

"When Things Go Wrong in Your Home It Should be No Surprise...They Always Give You a Warning." ~ Christopher Thomas

Updating/Maintaining Your Home

One day you will desire to sell that home that you've grown to love. You want your home to appreciate not depreciate. I always tell my homeowners, who will eventually become sellers to dig deep and think back to the time when they were searching for a home. What turned them off? What drew them in?

Most importantly, what was the deciding factor that led you to make an offer on that home?

Being a responsible homeowner will make your job as a seller easier when your time comes. Also, keeping track of major improvements such as roof, furnace, hot water tanks, and kitchen and bath updates will make your home more desirable when you decide to sell.

Cleaning and Inspecting the Furnace

Every 1-2 Years you should have a qualified HVAC technician clean and inspect your furnace and check the heat exchanger for any defects or cracks. Also, change your filters every 3-6 months depending on the thickness of the filter. (See HVAC.com for a reference on how often you should replace your filter). During the winter months when the furnace is working overtime you should change your filter **monthly**.

Cleaning Gutters and Downspouts

Gutters are designed to catch rainwater and carry it away from the foundation of the home through downspouts. At least once or twice a year, freeing your gutters of leaves and other debris will protect your home against water damage. Clogged gutters and downspouts cause water to damage your roof (causes leaks) and foundation (causing a leaky basement). Make sure that you add downspout extensions to carry water away from your home.

Maintain Trees and Shrubs Close to Your Home

Trees that overhang onto your roof and/or siding can increase the rate of deterioration of your roof or siding. They also create a way for pests or vermin such as squirrels, raccoons, or even birds to enter your attic or crawlspace. Trust me there is nothing like realizing that you have new non-human roommates living "rent-free" in your home. Removal of those pests can cost you hundreds, even thousands of dollars in the long run.

Depending on where you live it's also important to ensure that trees and limbs are far away from your home because they can cause more damage during an ice or windstorm.

Change your Smoke Detector Batteries

A good rule of thumb is to change your smoke detector batteries each season (summer, spring, winter, and fall). If you do not have smoke detectors, check with your local fire department, or purchase them at your local home improvement store.

Also, make sure that you have carbon monoxide detectors on each floor of your home especially near sleeping areas. Carbon monoxide is an odorless gas that can come from improperly vented appliances. Carbon monoxide displaces oxygen in the blood and deprives the brain, heart, and other vital organs of oxygen. It is very important to have a working carbon monoxide detector on the lowest level of your home (basement or bottom floor crawl space) because by the time carbon monoxide reaches the living or sleeping areas where you and your family are it will be too late.

This reinforces why it is so important when purchasing a home to have a licensed home inspector or engineer thoroughly inspect your home and appliances (gas stoves, furnaces, water heaters, wood-burning stoves, etc.) if they are a part of the purchase.

Make It Your Own

When it's all said and done, sit back and enjoy your accomplishment! Purchasing a home is one of the biggest purchases many of us will ever make in our entire lives. It is a luxury that is not afforded to everyone, although, we are fighting every day to change that. Take the time to settle in, enjoy being a homeowner, add those small touches that say, "I live here, and this belongs to me".

Wishing you Happy Home Shopping and All of Your Heart's Desires on your First Home!

Home Improvement Notes

_____

_____

_____

_____

_____

_____

_____

_____

_____

_____

_____

_____

_____

_____

_____

_____

_____

_____

_____

Ty's Most FAQ

How long have you been in the business?

I have been in the business for 11 years. I have been a licensed real estate agent (realtor) for 10 years and I went back to obtain additional credentials as a licensed real estate broker. I have been a broker for over two years. The primary difference between a real estate agent and broker is that a broker can own a real estate firm or hire agents to work for them.

Do you work independently or with a team?

All real estate agents are independent contractors. So, I have our own clients and run my own business, but I work under a broker/brokerage (Christopher Thomas, New 2 U Homes). If one of us is on vacation or unavailable we may rely on each other in an emergency; there are six current agents at New 2 U Homes, including myself.

What percentage of your business is working with homebuyers?

90%

How many buyers do you represent at a time?

It depends on whether it is the busy or slow season. Five is my comfort level although I have worked with up to nine buyers at once.

How many homes have you helped close in the past year?

New 2 U Homes helps 60-100 clients per year close on homes. I assist around 25 homebuyers, per year, close on homes, this does not include my listings.

How long is the process for a buyer to find and purchase a home?

The process varies by client. There is no specific length of time. Everyone does not come to New 2 U Homes pre-approved. This is what makes us different from the other brokerages. We assist our buyers from credit to closing and beyond. This is a more intense and extensive process than working with pre-approved buyers. My longest time from credit to closing with a buyer was 8-years and my shortest time was probably 30 days (cash deal).

Do you have a questionnaire for homebuyers?

No, I do not. I prefer getting to know my buyers through meeting them in person and organic interactions with one another.

In what neighborhood(s) do you specialize in?

I am a licensed real estate broker throughout New York State. I specialize in Rochester and its surrounding suburbs and counties.

What kind of guarantee(s) do you offer?

I do not offer any guarantees. I do not believe in forcing relationships, whether business or personal. I take pride in homing in on my clients' wants and assisting them with finding their home. If for some reason this doesn't happen, I can ask if they would like to work with another agent at New 2 U Homes or I can refer them to another brokerage.

What challenges do first-time homebuyers face?

There are always challenges and obstacles that we cannot foresee. One specific obstacle is utilizing grants (adds an additional 30 days onto a contract and has an additional inspection). A seller's market is yet another obstacle when sellers have a plethora of buyers at their fingertips overbidding on homes and at times even offering cash for a quick closing. Sellers may be more prone to select someone without a grant or someone who can get to the closing table quicker. I have had buyers who still overcame those odds because I am an agent skilled in handling grants. I know how to reassure the listing agent/realtor who may not be familiar with the grant aspect. I get my buyer through the process and to the closing table.

Will buyers be able to review documents ahead of time?

We are a technology-based brokerage and most of our documents are presented via email and electronically. Therefore, you will not only be able to receive documents ahead of time but also have copies at your fingertips for your records.

Who will be responsible for paying you? How much do you charge?

Our services are of NO COST to you as the buyer. The seller agrees to pay a commission for having their home sold. This commission is then shared between the listing agent and the agent who brings a qualified buyer (buyer's agent).

Do you assist with helping buyers locate other professionals?

New 2 U Homes is an all-inclusive real estate brokerage. I have a list of professionals that I have worked with to get my clients to the closing table (inspectors, attorneys, etc.).

What are five things that separate you from your competitors?

Experience, knowledge of grants, education & case management background helped me develop a holistic approach with my clients. I care about people, not the money. If it were just for the money I wouldn't get up in the morning and do what I do.

What are some things that give you an advantage over your competitors?

Being Ty Thomas :)

What are your expectations of your clients?

Everyone in the transaction has a job to do. I expect my clients to respond in a timely fashion because I extend the same courtesy. Additionally, a lack of a timely response can be the difference between them getting that home or missing out.

What else should readers know about yourself or New 2 U Homes?

I take immense pride in my name and my brand. I also take pride in the fact that New 2 U Homes is an independently owned African American brokerage. We have never worked under any other brokerage and we were the first African American brokerage to be recognized by the Greater Rochester Area of Realtors (2014) for obtaining platinum status (the highest level of sales achievement). We sold 100 homes in one year.

Share more about yourself.

I have Obsessive Compulsive Disorder (OCD) and love to travel :)

What do you pride yourself on?

Not being a procrastinator and being resourceful.

What is important to you?

Not having my time taken for granted and giving 100% to whatever I do.

What are your goals and ambitions?

To publish my First *Time Homebuyer Handbook*, to be a motivational speaker, and educator! To travel the world educating first time homebuyers and young, influential agents who put PEOPLE first.

Why did you get into real estate?

I obtained my real estate license in 2009 after leaving a career of teaching and helping troubled youth. I worked at the Action for a Better Community as a Head Start Teacher and the Urban League of Rochester as the Youth Intervention Program Coordinator. When my husband opened the brokerage in 2008, the year of the Obama

Homebuyer Tax Credit, there was a void that needed to be filled. After two years of being prayerful, I finally went full-time in real estate. I helped five first time homebuyers within months of obtaining my license purchase their first homes and have been doing that ever since.

What else would you like to share?

As an African American female in a predominately white male industry, I am constantly trying to prove myself. I must work 100 times harder, which comes naturally to me because I am a meticulous overachiever. I work fervently and passionately, regardless of my experience in the industry.

List additional questions you may want to ask your realtor.

_____

_____

_____

_____

_____

_____

_____

_____

_____

_____

_____

_____

_____

_____

_____

_____

Glossary

So, by the time you finish this section you will be an expert on what to look for when searching for a home. These are the various statuses and definitions that you may see when you are searching for a home:

Active-The home is currently listed for sale and available to view. In a seller's market you want to view homes quickly before the status changes.

Buyer's Market-The market is in the buyer's favor. There are a lot of homes available but not as many buyers looking.

Collection-debt owed by an individual to a creditor or lender.

Continue to Show Under Contract-The home has received and accepted an offer. Sellers continue to show the home and accept backup offers just in case the first offer does not pan out.

Contract-A written, legal contract between the buyer and seller once the seller accepts the offer. It will include price, terms, and pertinent information regarding deadlines that must be adhered to.

Earnest Money Deposit-a deposit a buyer makes on a home they want to purchase.

Encumbrance-a claim against a property by a party that is not the owner.

Expired-The home has been listed by a realtor; however, the listing has expired. The seller may or may not relist the home.

Foreclosure-the action of taking possession of a mortgaged property when the mortgagor (homeowner) fails to keep up their mortgage payments.

Homeowners Insurance-a form of property insurance that covers losses and damages to an individual's residence, along with furnishings and other assets in the home.

Inspection-When a licensed engineer or inspector does a detailed analysis of the home including electrical, plumbing, mechanical, and appliances if they are included in the purchase.

Inspection Fee-The fee that a licensed property inspector charges for determining the current physical condition of the property.

Judgment-an official result of a lawsuit in court. In debt collection lawsuits, the judge may award the creditor or debt collector a judgment against you.

Lien-a right to keep possession of property belonging to another person until a debt owed by that person is discharged.

Mortgage Appraisal Fee-The fee that a licensed property inspector charges for determining the current physical condition of the property.

Offer-A written, legal document in which the buyer makes an offer to the seller to purchase their home. It includes price and terms.

Pending-The home has received an offer and the process is pending. Perhaps the listing agent is still waiting for the buyer to release all their contingencies

(attorney approval, inspection, or mortgage commitment). Sellers are not accepting back up offers.

Seller's Market-The market is in the seller's favor. There are a lot of buyers looking but few homes are available, which can create a bidding war and drive the prices of homes above list price. You must have a savvy realtor that can move quickly and aggressively through this type of market.

Short Sale-a sale of real estate in which the net proceeds from selling the property will fall short of the debts secured by liens against the property. In this case, if all lien holders agree to accept less than the amount owed on the debt, a sale of the property can be accomplished. The homeowner is trying to avoid a foreclosure on their credit.

Withdrawn-The home has been taken off the market. The seller may have changed his or her mind about listing at this time or the market may have changed.

Most homebuyers want to know what to expect when venturing into the home buying journey. Remember, you must be pre-qualified or pre-approved before you make an offer on a property.

About the Author

Tysharda L. Johnson-Thomas

Associate Broker | New 2 U Homes LLC

Tysharda Johnson-Thomas graduated from Hampton University with a bachelor's degree in Psychology. After graduation she dedicated 14 years of her life to working with people between the ages of 3-21 years in a variety of capacities. She started her career in education as a preschool teacher (Action for a Better Community) and concluded it as a Program Coordinator for the Youth Intervention Program (Urban League of Rochester).

Mrs. Johnson-Thomas' next endeavor would be in the world of real estate. She joined her husband full-time in their real estate brokerage in 2009. New 2 U Homes was a mobile office for about four years. They realized that a central location was needed where their clients could come and get personal service. Since then Tysharda has helped New 2 U Homes grow tremendously, she specializes in listening to their buyers, finding the perfect home for them, and then negotiating the best deal possible. New 2 U Homes is a full-service real estate brokerage that assists their clients from credit to closing. They educate their buyers, assist with first time home buyers grant programs, and even attend most client closings. Tysharda and New 2 U Homes saw the need for first time homebuyers to have someone in their corner advocating on their behalf. They also saw that there was a great need for home buyer's education, advocacy, and just a familiar face to remain with them throughout the process.

Thanks to Tysharda' s dedication, leadership, and hard work, in November 2014 New 2 U Homes was recognized by the Greater Rochester Area of Realtors for obtaining platinum status (the highest level of sales achievement). They achieved their goal of becoming the first African American independently owned real estate brokerage in Rochester, NY to achieve platinum status.

Mrs. Johnson-Thomas loves seeing the faces and tears of her clients when she hands them their keys at the closing table. She is glad that she stepped out on faith and left a career that she had loved for so long to pursue something that she is now so passionate about.

Her advice to young hopeful entrepreneurs is to think of what you love doing the most and DO IT!

Additional Notes